POPULAR PET CARE

Dogs

Ann Larkin Hansen
ABDO & Daughters

Pets are more than just toys or playthings. They are part of our families. It is important to love and care for them. Popular Pet Care will help you understand your pet and know of its unique needs. Remember that your pet will depend on you to be responsible in caring for it.

Dr. David C. Hallstrom—Veterinarian

-Published by Abdo & Daughters, 4940 Viking Drive, Suite 622, Edina, Minnesota 55435.

Copyright © 1997 by Abdo Consulting Group, Inc., Pentagon Tower, P.O. Box 36036, Minneapolis, Minnesota 55435 USA. International copyrights reserved in all countries. No part of this book may be reproduced in any form without written permission from the publisher.

Printed in the United States.

Cover photograph by: Vik Orenstein
Interior Photo credits: Vik Orenstein
                        Peter Arnold, Inc.
                        Super Stock
Illustrations and Icons by: C. Spencer Morris
Edited by Julie Berg
Contributing editor Dr. David C. Hallstrom—Veterinarian

Special thanks to our Popoular Pet Care Kids:
        Peter Dumdei, Gracie Hansen, Brandon Isakson, Laura Jones, Annie O'Leary,
        Peter Rengstorf, Morgan Roberts, and Tyler Wagner

Library of Congress Cataloging-in-Publication Data

Hansen, Ann Larkin.
        Dogs / by Ann Larkin Hansen.
        p.   cm. -- (Popular pet care)
        Includes index.
        Summary: Suggests what to consider in choosing a dog for a pet: then offers advice on how to understand, train, feed, and generally care for this amazing creature.
        ISBN 1-56239-781-8
        1. Dogs--Juvenile literature. [1. Dogs. 2. Pets.] I. Title. II. Series: Hansen, Ann Larkin. Popular pet care.
        SF426.5.H36   1997
        636.7'0887--dc21   97-1593
                                                               CIP
                                                               AC

Contents

Why Have A Dog? 4

Which Dog Is Right For You? 6

Finding A Dog.. 8

Bringing A Dog Home 10

Feeding Your Dog 12

Exercise and Play 14

Grooming And Bathing 16

Training Your Dog 18

Housebreaking Your Dog 20

Going Through Life With Your Dog.................. 22

Spaying And Neutering 24

Keeping Your Dog Healthy 26

When Your Dog Gets Old 28

Glossary 30

Index 32

Why Have A Dog?

Are you looking for a best friend? A good dog will love you no matter what. A dog will snuggle with you while you watch TV. It will play with you and follow you anywhere.

But a dog needs more training and attention than any other pet. They need space and exercise. Some dogs need cold weather, and others need warm places. Some dogs are miserable if no one is home during the day.

Do you have the right house and enough time to make a dog happy? If you do, then you need to find the kind of dog that will make you happy.

Opposite page: Dogs need
a lot of attention.

Which Dog Is Right For You?

Every year thousands of dogs are left at **animal shelters** because their owners chose the wrong dog. Finding the right **breed** of dog is the most important part of having a dog.

There are more than 100 dog breeds, and each one is different. Some like to hunt, others like to pull sleds. Some dogs are born to herd sheep, or guard their owners. Some dogs are **mutts**, a mixture of breeds. Often mutts are healthier and happier than purebreds. Different breeds like different amounts of space and people. Call your **veterinarian** or go to the library to find what breeds of dogs might be happy with your house and family.

These dogs were bred to pull sleds.

Finding A Dog

Dogs and **puppies** can be found through ads in the paper, pet stores, dog **breeders**, neighbors, and **animal shelters**. Most people buy puppies. An older dog from an animal shelter is a good idea if you don't have a lot of time to train it.

When choosing a puppy or dog, first look at where they are living. Is it clean? Are the dogs well-cared for and happy? Meet the mother of the puppies. If she is friendly and well-behaved, the puppies should be also. Make sure the puppies are healthy and used to people. They should be between six and ten weeks old.

Opposite page: Two Labrador retriever puppies.

Bringing A Dog Home

Your **puppy** or dog will need a water dish and a food dish that won't tip over. Buy a leather or nylon **collar** and **leash**. Puppies grow very fast, so check the collar every week to make sure it isn't too tight. Puppies should have a pen or **kennel** in a busy place in the house. Use it for puppy naps, and when you are gone. But never leave a puppy alone in a kennel for a whole day. Would you like to be sent to your room for a whole day?

The puppy will be very lonely for its mother for a few nights. It will whimper and whine. Sometimes it is helpful to put a hot water bottle wrapped in a blanket in your puppy's sleeping place.

It's fun to bring home a new puppy.

Feeding Your Dog

A good brand of dry dog food keeps dogs' teeth and bodies healthy. **Puppies** need special puppy chow. They need to eat three or four times a day. Grown dogs just eat once each day. Follow the directions on the bag for how much and when to feed.

Dogs love treats, but chocolate and chicken bones can make them very sick. Cheese and cooked meats are good, and some dogs like vegetables. Don't feed your dog treats from the dinner table, or it will beg all the time. Dogs and especially puppies need things to chew. Give them beef bones or chew toys from the store. Be careful, some puppies can chew off large pieces of bone and get sick. Knotted nylon rope toys or nylon bones work well.

What you feed your dog is important.

Exercise and Play

Dogs need exercise, and they don't get it by themselves. Take your dog for a walk on a **leash** every day. Take along some plastic bags so that if it goes to the bathroom, you can clean up. Never leave a mess for someone else to step in!

Dogs love to play games. Fetch is always a favorite. Your dog chases a ball and brings it back to you. Some dogs will find toys that you hide. Many like to play tug-of-war with old towels. Try different games with your **puppy** to find what it likes best.

Opposite page: Dogs love to play and it's good for them, too!

Grooming And Bathing

Dogs get dirty. They like to roll in things and jump in lakes. Sometimes they get smelly from just being a dog.

Wash your dog in the bathtub or outside with buckets of **lukewarm** water. Scrub with a mild shampoo or dish soap, and rinse well. Have lots of towels, and dry the dog well before you turn it loose. Even then, it will probably shake water all over.

Dogs with long hair need to be brushed every day. Have your **veterinarian** show you how to clip your dog's nails. Check your dog often for dirty ears, runny eyes, cracked foot pads, and cuts.

Giving your dog a bath is important.

Training Your Dog

Dogs are part of the family, so they have to know the rules. Your dog must learn not to nip, jump on people, chase cars, chew on shoes, and to stay off the furniture. Your dog should also know its name and how to **come**, **sit**, **stay**, lie down, and **heel**.

Only train a **puppy** for a few minutes at a time. Show it what to do, and give lots of praise and petting when it does what you want. Once your dog learns that following **commands** makes you happy, it will work hard for you.

Many owners take their dogs to **obedience school** at about six months of age. Check your phone book for 4H clubs and dog trainers that teach classes.

Teaching your dog to sit.

Teaching your dog to lie down.

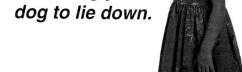

Reward your dog for good behavior.

Housebreaking Your Dog

Puppies must be trained to go to the bathroom outside. This may take three days to six months.

Every time the puppy wakes up or finishes playing, call it outside. Always go to the same place in the yard. Wait a few minutes. If the puppy goes, praise and pet it. If not, just take it back inside. Also, take the puppy out for ten minutes after every meal and before you go to bed. Never carry the puppy outside or it won't learn the way. In the evening, line the pen with newspapers for the puppy to use during the night.

If the puppy has an accident, never rub its nose in it. Just point at the mess and tell it, "bad dog." Soon the puppy will learn to whimper at the door when it needs to go out.

Housebreaking your puppy takes time and patience.

Going Through Life With Your Dog

As your dog ages it may become a little stiff and hard of hearing. Be sure your dog still gets plenty of love and has a soft, warm place to sleep.

A well-chosen, well-trained dog will be your best buddy for ten or more years. Dogs have lived closely with humans for thousands of years. They become a part of the family. Your company is what your dog wants most. Be your dog's leader and friend, and it will follow you anywhere.

Treat your dog like a friend.

Spaying And Neutering

Female dogs are **spayed** and male dogs are **neutered** to keep them from having **puppies**. There are many more dogs than there are homes, so thousands of dogs have to be put to death every year. Don't add to the problem with more puppies. Take your dog to the **veterinarian** before it is six months old for this operation.

After surgery, keep your dog from jumping or running too much. If the **incision** becomes red or swollen, call your veterinarian.

Opposite page: A vet with a dog after surgery.

Keeping Your Dog Healthy

Puppies need to have their first **vaccination** at eight weeks of age. They need a booster shot three to four weeks later, and a rabies shot at four months of age. Adult dogs should have booster shots once a year. This will protect them against many diseases.

Dogs should be checked for **worms** by your **veterinarian** twice a year. If your dog is outside a lot, you must watch for **ticks** and **fleas**. Ticks can be pulled off, but for fleas you will need a special shampoo or spray.

Never leave a dog in a car on a warm day, or it could die of heatstroke.

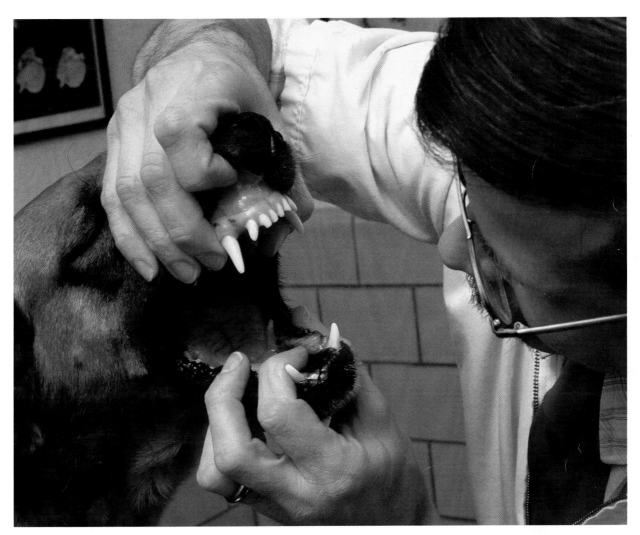

A vet checking a dog's mouth.

When Your Dog Gets Old

When your dog gets to be ten or twelve years old, it will start to slow down. It may not be able to walk as far, or jump up into the car. Many dogs get arthritis in their hips and knees. Some go deaf. They all need more sleep. Be sure to take especially good care of your friend at this time.

Your dog may finally just die peacefully in its sleep. But some dogs become so sick and miserable that the last favor you can do for them is have the **veterinarian** put them "to sleep." They are given a shot and die painlessly.

Burying your dog in a pet cemetery is very expensive. You could have your dog cremated, or the veterinarian can take care of the body for you.

It's sad to lose a pet, but you can be proud of yourself for giving your friend a happy life. And soon you may be ready for another pet!

A dog will always be your best friend.

Glossary

Animal Shelter: A home for unwanted animals. Shelters try to find new homes for these pets, but many animals have to be put to death because there is nowhere for them to go.

Breed: Different types of an animal. There is more variety in dog breeds than in any other type of animal. Also to raise or grow.

Collar: A band of leather or chain worn around the dog's neck.

"Come": The command used to call your dog to you.

Command: The words or hand signals used to tell a dog what to do.

Flea: A tiny, biting bug that lives on dogs and other animals. They will bite humans, too!

"Heel": The command used to make your dog walk at your side.

Incision: The cut made in the skin during an operation.

Kennel: A small cage for a dog to travel or rest in. A larger pen usually works better for a puppy.

Leash: A leather or nylon rope for hooking on the collar. This allows you to control the dog.

Lukewarm: Not hot and not cold.

Mutt: A dog with parents of different breeds. A mixed-breed.

Neuter: An operation done on a male dog to keep him from fathering puppies.

Obedience School: Classes that teach dogs to listen to and obey their owners.

Puppy: A dog less than one year old.

"Sit": The command used to make your dog sit down.

Spay: An operation done on a female dog to keep her from having puppies.

"Stay": The command to make your dog stay in place while you leave.

Tick: A blood-sucking insect.

Vaccination: A shot to protect against disease.

Veterinarian: An animal doctor.

Worms: Worms in animals live inside the animal and can make them ill. There are many different kinds.

Index

Symbols

4H club 18

A

animal shelters 6, 8
attention 4

B

bathing 16
bones 12
booster shot 26
breed 6, 8

C

collar 10
commands 18

D

disease 26

E

exercise 4, 14

F

family 6, 18
fetch 14
fleas 26
food 10, 12

G

games 14
grooming 16

H

heatstroke 26
herd 6
house 4, 6, 10
housebreaking 20
hunt 6

K

kennel 10

L

leash 10, 14
library 6
long hair 16

M

mutts 6

N

nails 16
neuter 24

O

obedience school 18

P

pet store 8
playing 14
puppies 10, 12, 18,
    20, 24, 26
purebreds 6

R

rabies 26
rules 18

S

sheep 6
sleds 6
spay 24

T

teeth 12
ticks 26
training 4, 20
treats 12

V

vaccination 26
veterinarian 6, 16,
    24, 26

W

worms 26